Your Moon

Ralph Angel

New Issues Poetry & Prose

A Green Rose Book

New Issues Poetry & Prose
The College of Arts and Sciences
Western Michigan University
Kalamazoo, Michigan 49008

First Edition, 2014.

ISBN: 978-1-936970-23-0 (paperbound)

Library of Congress Cataloging-in-Publication Data:
Angel, Ralph
Your Moon/Ralph Angel
Library of Congress Control Number: 2013949840

Editor: William Olsen
Managing Editor: Kimberly Kolbe
Layout Editor: McKenzie Lynn Tozan
Assistant Editor: Traci Brimhall
Editorial Intern: Dustin Brown
Art Direction: Nicholas Kuder
Design: Steven Miller
Production: Paul Sizer
                   The Design Center, Frostic School of Art
                   College of Fine Arts
                   Western Michigan University
Printing: McNaughton & Gunn, Inc.

This project is supported in part by an award from the National
Endowment for the Arts.

Your Moon

Ralph Angel

New Issues

WESTERN MICHIGAN UNIVERSITY

Also by Ralph Angel

Collections of Poetry:

Exceptions and Melancholies: 1986-2006
Twice Removed
Neither World
Anxious Latitudes
History, limited-edition chapbook

Translations:

Poem of the Deep Song (Federico García Lorca)

For Mary

Contents

Something will turn up.
—Roy Lichtenstein

The Wind Will Carry Us

for Abbas Kiarostami

Someone has been sleeping. Someone's
heading nowhere.

This is the winding road. Then there's a solitary
tree, and after that, nothing,
nothing.

If someone asks, say I'm
looking for buried treasure. Such a lovely
village. You've hidden it so well.

I haven't hidden anything. Our ancestors
built it here.

See that blue window, near the lady
sitting on the steps. Let's
go higher. I will

show you. Here's your
room.

We have a sack of apples. We have
fresh bread. You won't
get another chance

like this. On judgment day
it's obvious. I'm used to it. I work
here. If you stay a while longer, you'll
get used to it, too.

When I was little, and someone
told me a secret, I always wanted to reveal it.
And, eventually, I did.

"If you come into my house

oh kind one, bring me a lamp
and a window

through which I can watch the crowd
in the happy street."

I'm sorry to disturb you.

You're welcome.
This is my normal route.

Three Minutes and Sixty Years

A mere
shrug of atmosphere—
and then the fog
coughing up some buildings, and then
the smell of rain just inside
the door—
puts a naked eye
to things, and makes them
beautiful.

Losing
your phone is like
losing your mind. It's like
a fountain—
the door's wide open—
the words
tall buildings make
speak mostly to pigeons
and styrofoam
cups.

Get out.
Get out of my cab
he said. Wake up.
It's different.

Nude with Pebbles

Flowers fall. And I noticed
before I stood again and folded up the paper and rinsed my cup
their artifice. I myself

was fifty when I murdered, I don't know.
I'm here to break again my knuckles
or break them back. I'm here

to hate the wall and love especially the contours
of the coast and a city
further south.

For several moments more a deer looked at me
and ate some shrubs. And overhead
a raven

just like ravens do.

You are the shakes
and rhythm. You are the way that you've not seen before
that brings you

to yourself
again. A feeling digs you up, and look, the air is hung
with pictures. A nude

with pebbles. A nude with glass. A nude
unwrapping bandages.

The subject is a non-thing. I breathed
the sweetness of the air. Jasmine I could smell
and eucalyptus, olive trees

and cypress, an iron gate.
We are in our robes again, you won't remember.
You have found

a chicken sandwich. You are plotting out
your day. Maybe you'll go swimming. The bottom's
soft and old

and further out
the fields are screaming. Lazy yellow fields of sunflowers
in this dry heat, and you alone out there,

or rather, us.

Venetian Blind

At first you couldn't care less
but later on told me that you hadn't been out
except after dark
for a couple years or so.
I can't sleep

you said. Let me lay my head
upon you.

Me too
I said. I'm always hungry. The café wasn't
very full. When your
mind's made up

there's no one
talking.

But that's just it
you said. I

wasn't.

You're the Rub

Murmured in loneliness, round and round.
Let's not go inside. The cliffs drop off, and the ocean's
a friend—on the boardwalk
enough people alone
have died.
So relax, take your feet
off—nobody's
missing. There are many parts
of the mind. On that old
open day we let out our long green grass. A night's passed
and you expected it
to be there.
You're the rub—the love
that loves the love. I like especially the puddles
and your wire. I like your mud.
I like your part
of it.

Chinese Umbrella

You're right
of course about the ordinary emotions. The larger
our hearts were the more tranquil
the flight. A handful
of people pushed past us

into the terminal. We grabbed
a cab there and
cuddled.

For the rest of my life
I loved the high ceilings and the sweating
fires. The sun
blooms

in the water. It's cold there
and fabulous.

For the rest of my life
my eyelids were broken. The curtains
are thin. There's

bread in the market and whatever
the boats

bring.

In short I am making adjustments.
You on a tiled

bench in the courtyard. You stepping
off of a Vespa. You
under a Chinese
umbrella.

Now we're in a noisy
restaurant at night. You are luminous
and warm

and I am afraid again.

Don't leave
I say You shake your head

a little and lean
closer. I want you to stay
I say

but you still can't
hear me

and never
will.

Tested Here on Earth

Tonight, brief as it is, the wind has met the leaves. Your moon is
      mostly red and anxious. There's no way out. Behind this
      window, songbirds

flit about the tapestries. Like you, they welcome sleeplessness and
      understand the future. Like you, they sing and sing and
      sing.

Tonight, brief as it is, the wind calls out. Behind this window, the
      wayside never answers. Spring came sliding

up the scaffolding, and the angels at the top burn perfectly. My
      voice doesn't weigh a thing. Tonight, the night's

thrown down. I accept the challenge. Hello, nature,

you want to kill me.

Conversation

So I took a walk
inside. You're alone
when morning
comes.
Watching you sleep in
is better

than oatmeal,
even Irish
oatmeal,
that thing you do
so well.

When you were a fish
you were a salmon.
I know, I'm
slow, I
know.

November's a nice day
to be. The ocean's
near.
Your fog
is

everywhere.

So I
talked to I, I said
fuck death, everyone
I meet knows
someone

I know. I said
it's nice to be happy,

but no one
believes
me.

Take your time,
my love. The logs have lit
the fire.
The sweet scent
of your hair

kisses
my mouth, and I
kiss you back,
and pour
the tea.

Gall

Some other
time white feathers

blow all across
the lawn.

We get up
when we want to. We're

high on the hill.
I suppose

one has to be really out of it
for a while

to taste the love
that lags

behind
us. What else do we want

to be? Walking
hand in hand

in a garden we've yet to
experience?

In the tenderest
humidity. In the cicada's

persistence. Our love
a laurel

on the surface
of a pool.

Now

Were you guilty of something
your story would wear a black suit
and come to an end.
I leave you alone.
I mop up the afterlife
and slick back
its hair.

The sun blows so hard
the leaves have returned to their trees.
Their eyes are wide open.
Saltwater fish
slide

through the streets.

The pedestrian said there was sad
and oh how it would be
more interesting
to paint

her skin and hair.

Were I naked now
and am.

Three Figures

This morning I'm savoring
a taste of apricot in the air. Out of respect or gratitude
I suppose, for I would remember a nightmare
and have to utterly-shattered tell it to more than one person
so that it might come to mean that I'm free
finally of another disgusting
dead thing of me, I step down from my lovely bed
into a foreign country. Out of respect
no doubt, for the sweet air crowded with people
and traffic and the dog that fumbles
with a newspaper before sitting down to read it
at the edge of the square
where everything you forgot or might need
is spread out on the pavement.
I'll never tell you
about the time I suffered most. What's most painful
is most hidden, even from me. Anyway, there's
nothing I can do about it. It emerges
here and there, I'm sure, and you could find it
if you want to. If moseying
around the breads and watercolors
and vegetables and necklaces is somehow running away
from myself, it doesn't bother me. In that second
before waking there were three figures,
children, maybe, a boy
and two girls, maybe my sisters
and me, with their backs
to the city, staring at the water.
I like to think of it
that way.

Face

A completeness in itself,
                    the sky a blue fruit.

Shadows flew,
            and as the doves come back to her, and children
run to her, you could see a happy woman there,

and her deep sorrow.

Only love, and pain in the eyes of the waiter.
                              How fragile the
passersby, we're all dolled-up today,

how changeable.
            What you were telling me about
                             in my heart,
but sweet-smelling and fragrant, my crime

is hidden. Why else would I feel so guilty,
                        or your beauty
      punish me?

All you do is love me.

Tame Me

But how to get through to a mind
that's covered with rubbishy thoughts?
Not by thinking, that's
for sure. And that's the problem,
I think. In silence, and
stoned to death.

Oh it has a story, the silence.
It's musical and bright. Stuff moves
forward in it, but isn't it.
Thinking, thinking, the word itself
chipping into it. Morning
and raining, but not
so much. The sprouting stops
and starts again. Death's
vegetable.

Thinking, thinking. The wind
leans this way and that. My before
and my after. There should be a fat robin
for the worm at the back
of my throat. The moss growing
in dank places, I can
smell it. The first
sounds of garbage trucks
climbing the hill.
Oh Friday of loneliness
and fear. Oh worked-up Friday.
Thinking, thinking, the word itself
banging into the unsaid
so that I might
hear it.

Panic

In one breath of air
I swam to the bottom of the ocean and brought back the earth.

I painted the walls and the ceiling an even white.
Then I knocked out a wall.

On the lake a swan folds herself into her wings
forever. It was that

time of year. The snakes are making rain.

Untitled

for W.S. Merwin

In which neither of us moved
whether we both were a dream
listening to the river
and there stayed without moving
your long amber curls
flowing beyond the dark trees
with its porch and grey-painted floorboards
that I'd always known
sitting on the steps
of that cabin

Please wait a while longer
if you are able to
keep the colors of sunlight
taking into themselves
the leaves here and there begin
small flocks of birds
a day after the full moon
the late roses and
vast scent

I was not born here
in the cold morning
that's hidden in their calls
I know where they are the birds
that are empty
the dumbest
of water
runs in the mind
flashing its colors
and in the sound of the breathing
answering it

the love you know
without end in the dark
sleep softly my love
in the night where
you go

You know there was never
in the small hours
awake above the still valley
in your words
clear and unseen
another sky
all through the day
you can tell
that side of darkness
what could be known at the time
and survived beyond
ever arriving

Willing

And further in...the train clacking and lulling...

rolling green hills coming toward us...

a perfect cloud shadow,
the lonely oaks.

And cows, one, and another, closer to heaven...
what's up with that?

A kiss, a lick, "Miss me?"
"Of course, yes,"

you're killing me here, my
dear. "Hungry?" "Brilliant, yes,

absolutely." "And voila," a nudge, a squeeze...
my stockinged foot curled

around your ankle, your shoulder
propped up on mine,

"we have grapes and brie, will you tear us
some bread?" A kiss, a lick,

"Miss me?" "Yes, yes." "I put your book
with the magazines."

"Perfect, brilliant. Might I have another?"
"Another what?"

Agnes

Here comes perfection. When I think of art I think of beauty. I
put my arm around it. Around my mind, I mean.

You may as well give up judging what you've done. The day is
young, the grey sun stayed that way.

Here comes an iron shade, partly down. Their heads are gone.

Please don't print the negative. I love their shoes. It's where the
light is.

The Traffic Is Going down the Hills

The traffic is going down the hills
above the city to the harbor

and back again, past the statue
of a goddess poised

in her abandon. Her arms
hang to the side

without touching her body.

At her feet a beautiful young girl
holds a plastic bag

in her hand, ready to pick up
her pet's

droppings.

Little sister, arranging
bottle caps. Little brother, back

and forth you run
from one side of the pier

to the other.

Oh young mother
pulling your thin dress

to yourself
tighter

and tighter.

What's Fair Is Fair

The police didn't do anything to them. Legs in stockings

with flowers. Windows and plants. The potting shed. Some
       children have to run away in the middle of the night

to join the circus. Some people stand around forever it seems
       alongside the airport conveyor belt. Here in the tissue
       paper

silence and sunlight flap their wings.

The god who wanted to be a truck driver

takes out a fruit stand. He knows what you're thinking. The
       traffic's bad. Take the money

bunny. What are you wearing.

The weather's old and personal. It doesn't

have an end. That's

the bottom line.

Erasure

for Natsume Soseki

I don't want you to know about any of this. I probably changed.
        I was invariably disgusted with myself.

Then she began to talk deliriously. She lost her power of speech.
        When I got home she laughed.

I who had not remembered. What one says and what one thinks
        are entirely different things. Every time I go outside

this is the price I paid.

It's blood that moves the body. Words aren't meant to stir the
        air only. They see somewhere in my heart

so long as my wife's
alive.

Other Means

All those notebooks aren't really necessary.
I behaved most awkwardly.
The sea came in and the cold just
disappeared there.
I remember when but don't know how the kissing
started. We hugged
ourselves and hugged the shore.
Or there you are

and how you came
to hate me. Or how ideas
come to me.
I kissed the stone and the newly buried
bones beneath us
and die
convinced of that. Don't
you?

It's nutty raining
here.

Holding You Sober Close to Me

The city's
behind us. The water's calm. There are many heads
above the water.

Show me a victim and I'll show you
a bathroom—a man slathered
in honey, a carpet

of flies.

Orange blossoms
and salt. Even the creepy doorman
tastes the salt

in the air.

If a child's brought in, well, that's something
different. We don't want
our animals

to suffer.
You're the last person on earth
prepared for the death

of your parents.

Nature

Looking through trees strangely into nature.

A window, an air-conditioner, a wall covered with ivy.

The book on your lap. Your head tilted back.

Like handling cups or pennies, a shovel, a stone.

Like where an arm is found, or where the tangled limbs go.

A bookshop, a fruit stand. You wake up and there you are, and
there you are.

"Do we have any cookies, or something nice?"

Toward the east outstretches the shadow. On the left a plywood
lake.

Gods and horses playing in the fountain. A conch shell. A robe.

The swallows, the sandstorms, a pink fire in the clouds.

And the generator, the chain and the pulley. Unheard-of laughter
and prayer.

The long exhalation. Of baskets and flutes.

Of bracken. Of reed. Of cypress and olive, pelvis and spine.

Three shoes on a doorstep. Of human unfinished.

The spirit in time.

All Night Long

All night long the moon is wandering behind the clouds
and upon the water. All night the flickering

in shop windows across an empty street, in the small
café that won't open for hours, if at all

today, where fish skins have yet to be swept
from the floors and the air is stale

with drink. All night long
the faint outlines of faces you've loved

and forgotten, and a bicycle
tied to a tree. A rat plops from a fence

and if you listen carefully you might hear
the first stirrings in the harbor

or the cry of the gulls
and catch yourself mumbling

and not know who in the world
you are talking to.

Bright Example

A few stones, day after day, dreamily
walked beside me. Houses
and trees and bright red
orioles, if I think
back on it, in their privacy.
For now, the elm trees
swarm with bees. Their hum
could keep me
there. Your
sky is blue and huge
and open.

I think about
the locals. Like people
screaming. I think it's a dog he's
carrying, but it's a paper bag.
She stays closer
to the gravel. She leans
against it, but
prefers the wooden fence.
Another car turns
over. Another
sputters.

And you, my dear
skeleton, in your pajama
bottoms, say
hello to everyone.
Another rock. A plastic
rose. Toy animals, can you believe it,
a flag, a poem.

But Not in Life

So we just ate sand

Then someone walks in
and looks around
and sees
someone else
and then walks over
and has
something
to say

You do it alone
whatever
it is

A hotel painted gray
turned-blue
all over
the
place

Hurrah the love
lost out
of it

Hurrah
your spirit
there

Make
a prayer

Blue Hydrangea

Five trucks are enough.
The neighbors
are home. We're married

and handsome
and covered. Nobody
dies

for the first time.
I'm still
fighting you.

You wait on me. I wait on
you. Your memory's
my body's

devotion.

Green Yarn

There are streets
there are wires
there is a
broken curb
"ouch"—your word
not mine, my
mouth your one
vocal-chord
raspily
sexy from
my lips
voice!

And when you
roll over
on to your
side and stretch
your legs just
so—so that
your toes point
away from
it all—it
all goes "boink"
in the sand
and the blue
sea even
the lesser
blue sky too
is beside
itself!

　　　—"floatingly,"
my love, that's
what I say
when the mind
goes away
pelicans
make a line
of their own

across the
emptiness
a couple
wet frisky
dogs leap through!

Such easy
privacy
you and me
in public
places
especially
          —you leaning
your head on
my shoulder
fast asleep,
me with a
map in hand
and also
asleep—will
we be on
this blanket
forever!

Being Back

Sooner or later I am out folding chairs again, and so
leave myself behind, though flirting
with an angel a few stairs
above me
feels just as real
and keeps things moving.

A golden retriever licks my hand. It's Christmas
in Chicago. The family's here
and from the cemetery
there's talk of food
and family.

It's flat
and cold in Dallas. And then a bursting
cloud of grackles.

An old man pees himself. His wife
takes her seat and thanks me. In Louisville,
Kentucky, a baby's
handed me.

In Seattle (must I go there, too?), I'm here
for you, and I know

I won't be back.

Fear of Death

Be pleased then, living one,
                                    from the balcony
that's what you're doing.

You never do
              how things were when you were a child
try.

I myself stand turned to the wind
                              higher and higher
and one day
              oh one day.

A cat steps up from your lap
                                    onto the tabletop.
You're in your yellow
                  sun dress
against the light.

Now I've put
              my brick-framed window
against the pane
              behind you.

The palms are nice.
                  As is the latticework

(is that jasmine?)
              for your protection.

And next to the bowl of plums

                                        a small bronze coffee pot
        right where your hand
                                is nearly touching it.

        Yes,
                it's the best spot
                                        and exactly where to stop.

Anne Frank

The function of the door is to protect us.

This is the earth we came out of. The smell is everywhere. Even
 after washing my hands, I see the glitter.

Buildings, too, have voices. The city an accumulation of memories
 handed down from one building to another.

The child does not understand how to please the mother or the
 father.

From my room, I see the whole graveyard.

My mind is empty. My heart a sweet earthy smell. My mind is
 listening for voices that might heal your hardships and
 calm your fears.

I start small. I start with the idea of freedom.

Skin

You're tired. You're
troubled. Your
skin's gone
thinner. When
you died
I became
you.

Everyone's
got to be
somewhere. What
were we there
to be.

The Heckler

His eyes were so good
he could see flies
fucking.
Depression lasts
as long as
the metaphor.
Now
a butterfly
comes in.
What do we do
with it?
Oh, it's already
gone.

Vacuum Cleaner

I erased the message. You were
already on your way. I barely heard you
pull the scent out of my ear
and put it in my
mouth again, where
I will kiss you.

Then I knocked over my café con leche.
What a mess. Papers, piles
of books, I had a book
in my hand.

I like it better now,
the table. The light cuts right
through. I think you'll
like it too.

Last night I woke myself up
in a sea of popcorn. The movie
had long since
ended. It was disgusting.
So we've got clean
sheets.

If only I had a little more
time. I take that back. I really
mean it. I wish
we hadn't yelled goodbye

last time. I mean we
really screamed it.

No wonder there was a beautiful
fish in the market. The sky
dimmed the living room. And peonies
opened. No wonder
the cat's lounging on the edge of the tub
while I'm making myself
presentable. She
makes it look
easy.

Only Quiet

Only quiet
as even a soft rain
quiets the city
even my thinking
while my neighbor
plays the piano
and a finch
awakens

Not so much
the idea of the past
but in hope
that it goes
away

We met long ago
and so begin
to meet
again

Speak kindly the sad song
written for no one

Talking Smack with Saints

You can be yourself now, and children playing after supper
have made the last cut diagonally of sun

across the plaza.
Like standing at attention among the flapping pigeons, or sitting

back to coffee
and talking smack with saints and smoking, the fountains

have been blasted, the gardens
duly groomed.

A train will come. And when it comes the difference
between the story of your life

and the damage
off the coast sleeps upon eternity, whose neck and head

have broken off, and you're
feeding it.

Dying

Did I cry? Did I fret?
Did I drive into an underground garage
like this, and swallow the dead air, and come out
with dahlias?
Did the heat never break suddenly like this
into calm enough, calm enough,
every day of my life

did I not get down on the dirt like this
and make it deeper?
Did my fingers tingle? Did my shoulder
numb? Did I feel even once
an old insanity pressing
down on my brain

and with a short stick
turn the turd over, and yell at it?
Did I not light a match, or
nudge a sapling, or reach for the heavens
like this, and bend

over backwards a new face with the sun
in the water, and, just like this,
stand on one foot
and lose a little breath
for a man with a lot of time
on his hands?

What I'm Thinking

The great fires have lit.

On the head of a bald man the story's been told.

More difficult were the paintings, which required a warehouse
and many assistants.

I never know what I'm thinking until I see what I've done, and
then have to do it all over again.

Shrubs of a feather get together, and that's

what I'm working on.

No birds.

Hunker down. The gnats here

bite in the morning. We're building new bodies

all the time.

Afar

Trees laced and bare
against the sky. The sky. A few green leaves
against it.
The light is night. In the city one steps over all sorts
of things. Twenty-six
birds
in the mail. It's breezy
cold. In hell they die in summer homes
above their
diaries.

The suicides
especially should not bother you. We like
the shitty squad cars. People
crowd the photo booth
so that it might be
said.
And if you're nuts you'll edit this
so as not to overwhelm
your body from
afar.

Acknowledgments:

Grateful acknowledgment is made to the following publications in which the poems of *Your Moon* first appeared:

The American Poetry Journal, Bat City Review, Burnside Review, The Café Review, Connotation Press, The Harvard Review, The Laurel Review, LIT, Numero Cinq, Pleiades, Plume, Redivider, 2nd and Church, Smartish Pace, Spillway, Tuesday; An Art Project, Verse Daily, Volt, Washington Square, The Yale Review

"What's Fair Is Fair" also appeared in *Breaking the Jaws of Silence: Sixty American Poets Speak To the World*, University of Arkansas Press

"Only Quiet" also appeared in *Live Life: The Daydreamer's Journal*, NinjaKnight Productions and Publishing

"Agnes" is for Agnes Martin; "The Heckler" is for Mary Ruefle; "Anne Frank" is for Louise Bourgeois, Tadao Ando, and Nora Naranjo-Morse; "Nature" is for Steve Reich

With special thanks to Virginia Campbell. And to Connie, David, Marcus, and Mary.

photo by Mary Cahill

Ralph Angel's *Exceptions and Melancholies: Poems 1986-2006* received
the 2007 PEN USA Poetry Award, and his *Neither World* won the
James Laughlin Award of The Academy of American Poets. In addition
to five books of poetry, he also has published an award-winning
translation of the Federico García Lorca collection, *Poema del cante
jondo / Poem of the Deep Song.* Angel is the recipient of numerous
honors, including a gift from the Elgin Cox Trust, a Pushcart Prize,
a Gertrude Stein Award, the Willis Barnstone Poetry Translation Prize,
a Fulbright Foundation fellowship and the Bess Hokin Award of the
Modern Poetry Association. He lives in Los Angeles, and is Edith
R. White Distinguished Professor at the University of Redlands,
and a member of the MFA in Writing faculty at Vermont College
of Fine Arts.

The Green Rose Prize

2013:   Ralph Angel
        Your Moon

2012:   Jaswinder Bolina
        Phantom Camera

2011:   Corey Marks
        The Radio Tree

2010:   Seth Abramson
        Northerners

2009:   Malinda Markham
        Having Cut the Sparrow's Heart

2008:   Patty Seyburn
        Hilarity

2007:   Jon Pineda
        The Translator's Diary

2006:   Noah Eli Gordon
        A Fiddle Pulled from the Throat of a Sparrow

2005:   Joan Houlihan
        The Mending Worm

2004:   Hugh Seidman
        Somebody Stand Up and Sing

2003:   Christine Hume
        Alaskaphrenia
        Gretchen Mattox
        Buddha Box

2002:   Christopher Bursk
        Ovid at Fifteen